HOW TO DRAW A NORMAL CURVE ON A HISTOGRAM

USING FREE SCIENTIFIC CHARTING SOFTWARE

WALTER EBNER

INNOVEASE

Every effort has been made to make this book as complete and accurate as possible. However, this book is supplied "as is" and without warranties. All warranties, express or implied, are hereby disclaimed. Furthermore, neither the publisher nor the author accepts any liability whatsoever for actions or consequences the reader may take or incur as a result of reading the information contained herein.

PUBLISHED BY:
Innovease
12 Pine Road
Malvern, Pennsylvania
19355

CONTENTS

INTRODUCTION

As a scientist, I love to graph data. Over my career, I've drawn thousands of scatter graphs and regression curves.

And when I'm doing statistical studies, I like to draw histograms with overlaid normal curves to see how my data are distributed. Unfortunately, programs like Excel are not well suited to draw graphs with two line types and statistical packages generally produce ugly graphs. The latter graphs are OK for viewing the data on a computer screen but not for publishing in an article or report.

I am very fussy about the quality of graphs I produce and want them to both look good and to clearly convey the message I am trying to present. In my opinion, ugly graphs just don't cut it.

After getting frustrated with the graphing options available to me for generating histograms with an overlaid normal curve, I decided to develop the capabilities to generate these graphs myself. I thought this would be a one or two hour exercise. Unfortunately, that was a gross underestimation!

But I was persistent. Here is what I've come up with.

CHAPTER 1

Charting Software

Microsoft Excel is generally the software one first turns to for data analysis and graphing. And it is quite versatile for this purpose, capable of doing a wide range of data analyses and drawing a wide variety of graphs, including histograms.

The Data Analysis Add-in is needed to draw histograms in Excel, but this is easy to download and install. However, the histograms in Excel do not allow the drawing of a scatter graph on top of a histogram. Although this restriction can be overcome with a lot of trickery or additional add-ins, this was not an approach I wanted to pursue.

And now, being retired, I no longer have access to commercial statistical programs. But that was OK because I never liked the graphs they generated anyway.

I decided the way to go was to use scientific charting software. The best program of this type I've ever used was Origin by OriginLab Corporation. I absolutely love this program. But it is very expensive and I just couldn't afford it now that I was retired. So I started looking around at open source scientific charting programs and stumbled across QtiPlot.

QtiPlot is designed to be an Origin clone. It's a little clunky and doesn't offer all the features of Origin, but, overall, it does a good job and is the best open source program of this type that I've found to date.

QtiPlot is the program I now use for histograms with an overlaid normal curve.

QtiPlot can be downloaded for free at:
https://www.zwodnik.com/software/windows/qtiplot

The program requires Python27.dll to run, which can be downloaded for free here: *http://www.dll-files.com*

QtiPlot is not installed like other programs. Just put the Python27.dll file in the same directory as qtiplot.exe and then double click on qtiplot.exe whenever you want to run it. Like I said, a little clunky, but it works well.

CHAPTER 2

Data Set

The data set selected for to demonstrate my graphing technique was taken from: Stuart L. Meyer, *Data Analysis For Scientists and Engineers*, Table 7.4, p. 25, 1975.

The demonstration data set has 51 data points representing individual length measurements of an unidentified object, expressed in cm. The measurements are as follows:

Table A1: The Demonstration Data Set Consisting Of 51 Length Measurements in cm

10.1	10.4	10.5	10.7	10.9
10.2	10.4	10.5	10.7	10.9
10.2	10.4	10.5	10.7	11.1
10.2	10.4	10.5	10.7	
10.3	10.4	10.6	10.7	
10.3	10.4	10.6	10.7	
10.3	10.5	10.6	10.7	
10.3	10.5	10.6	10.8	
10.3	10.5	10.6	10.8	
10.3	10.5	10.6	10.8	

10.4	10.5	10.6	10.8	
10.4	10.5	10.7	10.9	

The mean of the data set is 10.54 and the standard deviation is 0.2127. The range of the data is from 10.1 to 11.1.

CHAPTER 3

Drawing a Histogram In QtiPlot

To draw a histogram in QtiPlot, open the program and paste the data to be used for the histogram into the 2(Y) column of Chart Table 1. Pasting is done using "Ctrl-V" or through the top menu: "Edit \ Paste Selection."

Select the data in Column 2(Y) of Chart Table 1 by clicking on the top header cell where "2(Y)" is displayed. When selected, the data will be highlighted. From the top menu, select: "Plot \ Statistical Graphs \ Histogram." This will create the histogram chart.

If necessary, change the scale of the x-axis by double clicking on one of the numeric labels on the axis. This opens the "General Plot Options" dialog box. In the dialog box, click on the "Scale" tab then on the "Bottom" button on the left side of the dialog to select the bottom axis. Now, adjust the "From" and "To" values as appropriate. Click the "Apply" button at the bottom of the dialog to apply the changes.

From this dialog box, you can also change other aspects of the graph's appearance including grid lines, axis tic marks, axis font size, font type, etc. for any of the chart axes. Once you are satisfied with the appearance of the graph, click "OK" at the bottom of the dialog to close it.

To change the number of columns in the histogram, you must change the bin width used by QtiPlot to create the chart. Decrease the bin width to add more columns and increase it to reduce the number of columns.

The bin width is changed by double clicking on the top of the tallest column in the chart to open the "Plot Details" dialog box. Click on the "Histogram Data" tab, uncheck the "Automatic Binning" checkbox, and enter the desired bin width in the "Bin Size" field. Click "Apply" to redraw the chart then click "OK" to close the dialog box. Bin width and how to calculate it will be discussed in more detail later on.

Figure 1 shows the histogram that we will be using for our example in this discussion, created from the demonstration data set given in Table A1 using 9 bins and a bin width of 0.11. The x-axis is scaled from 9.5 to 11.5.

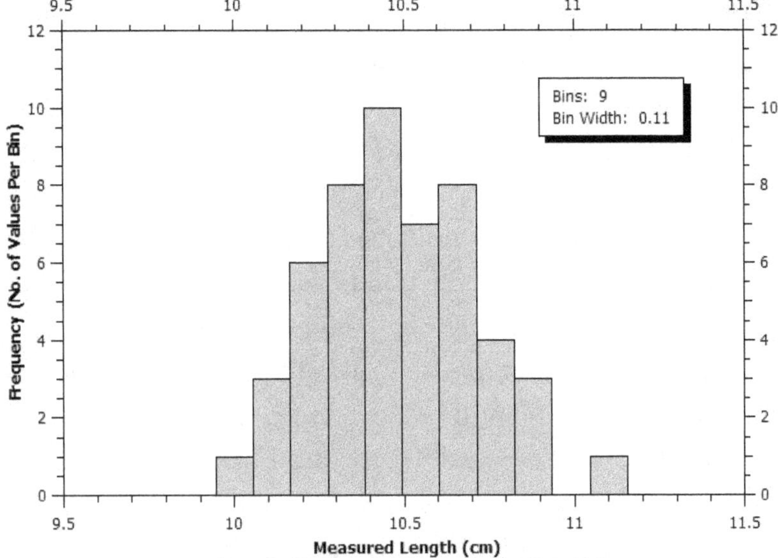

Figure 1. Histogram of Demonstration Data Set

CHAPTER 4

Printing and Exporting Charts In Qtiplot

Once you have completed a chart, you will want to print it or export it (i.e. save it) so you can use it in a publication. Charts are exported as image files.

To print a chart, click on the top of the chart to select it and then select "File \ Print" from the top menu and then click on the "Print" button in the "Print" dialog box that opens.

To export a chart, click on the top of the chart to select it and then select "File \ Export Graph \ Current..." from the top menu. This opens the "Choose a Filename to Save Under" dialog box.

Navigate to the folder where you want the chart saved, enter a file name for the chart, and then select a file type. For most cases, JPG or PNG files are preferred.

Adjust the Image Quality and/or Print Resolution (DPI) if desired. For most cases, the default values are just fine.

If desired, the size of the saved chart can be changed by checking the "Custom print size" checkbox and filling in the "Unit," "Width," Height," and "Scale Fonts Factor" fields reflecting the new size desired. For most purposes, the default size is satisfactory.

Once the parameters have been set, click the "Preview" button to see how the saved chart is going to look. Click on the "X" in the red box at the top right of the preview window to exit the preview window when finished.

To export the chart, click the "Save" button on the "Choose a Filename to Save Under" dialog box.

The saved chart can now be imported into Word, PowerPoint, or other program to use in a presentation or publication.

I often like to import the charts into PowerPoint and then print them from there. In that way, I can easily resize the image to make it fill a page and add a caption to describe the chart.

CHAPTER 5

Selecting the Optimal Number Of Bins For a Histogram

The purpose of a histogram is to display the distribution of numerical data to provide an estimate of whether or not the data are normally distributed. That is to see if the data reasonably fit the normal distribution curve.

When plotting a histogram, the data are grouped together according to their values and the number of values in each group is plotted as a vertical column on the chart. The data groupings are called bins and the width of each bin is called the bin width. Typically, all of the bins on a histogram are the same width.

The number of bins used can significantly change the shape of a histogram. Therefore, the number of bins is a critical factor when creating a histogram. Too few bins and the shape of the distribution is obscured. Too many bins and the distribution looks ragged.

There are several numerical methods to estimate the optimal number of bins for a histogram. However, this is not an exact science and the resulting values are only estimates that provide a good starting point for setting up the histogram. The visual appearance of the histogram is always the final selection method.

Here are two of the more popular numeric methods of estimating the optimal number of bins:

Sturge's Rule:

This method works best for data that are continuous, normally distributed, and symmetrical. It doesn't work well for skewed data.

The number of bins is calculated as follows

$$Bins = 1 + 3.22 * LOG(N) \qquad [1]$$

where

Bins = Number of bins

N = Total number of values in the data set

For our data set of 51 values, Sturge's Rule yields:

Bins = 1 + 3.22 * LOG(51) = 6.5 = 7 (rounded up since an odd number of bins generally works best)

Rice's Rule:

Rice's Rule is defined as follows:

$$Bins = 2 * \sqrt[3]{N} \qquad [2]$$

For our data set, the number of bins is calculated to be:

$$Bins = 2 * \sqrt[3]{51} = 7.4 = 7$$

Visual Observation Of the Histogram:

Once the optimal number of bins has been calculated, plot a histogram and see how it looks. Then vary the number of bins higher and lower than the calculated estimate to see how the histogram changes. Select the number of bins that shows the best distribution of the data.

As discussed earlier, QtiPlot uses bin width to set up a histogram. However, in general, it's easier to think in terms of the number of bins rather than bin width, in which case the bin width must be calculated. This is easily done by dividing the range of the data set by the number of desired bins, e.g.

$$BW = \frac{(n_{max} - n_{min})}{Bins} \qquad [3]$$

where

BW = Bin Width

n_{max} = The maximum value in the data set

n_{min} = The minimum value in the data set

Bins = The number of desired bins

For the demonstration data set, the bin width would be calculated as follows:

$$BW = \frac{(11.1 - 10.1)}{Bins} = \frac{1.0}{Bins}$$

Following are histogram charts that show the demonstration data set plotted with bin widths based on 5, 6, 7, 8, 9, 10 and 11 bins.

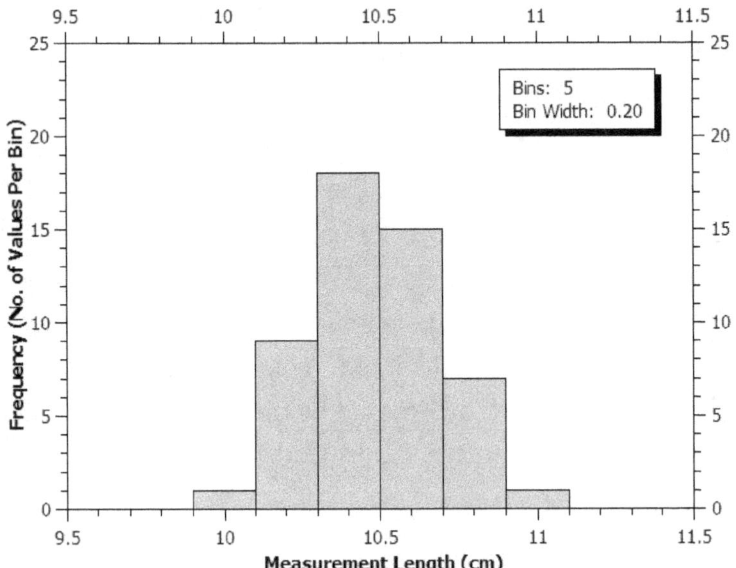

Figure 2. Histogram of Demonstration Data Set

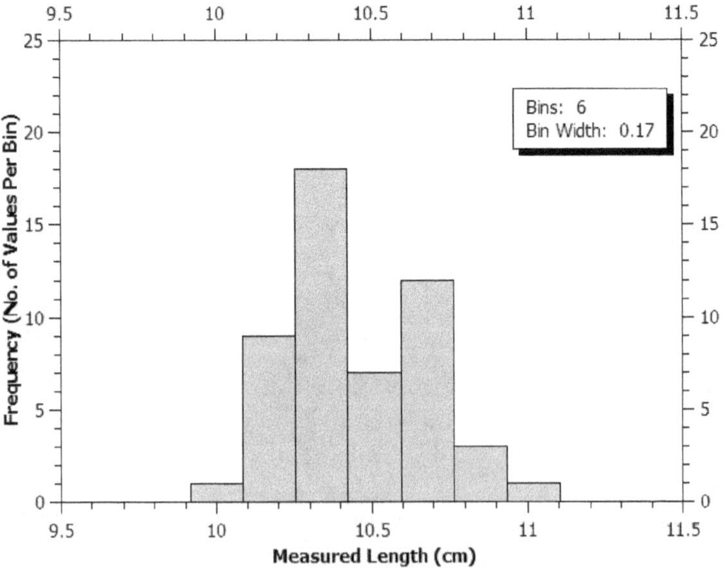

Figure 3. Histogram of Demonstrated Data Set

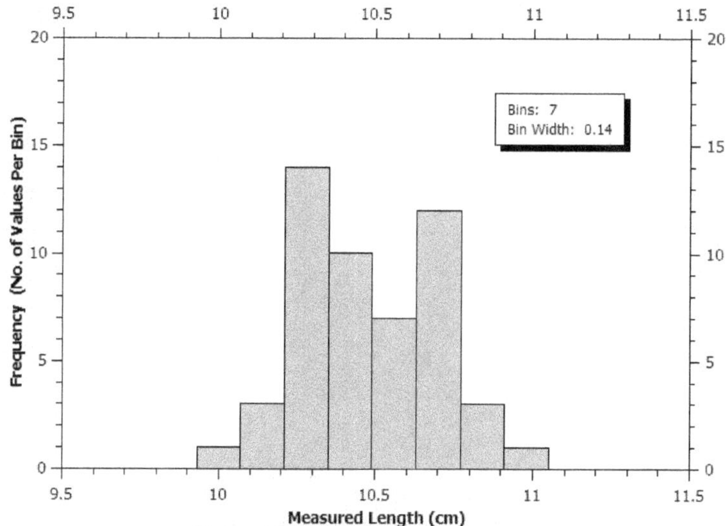

Figure 4. Histogram of Demonstration Data Set

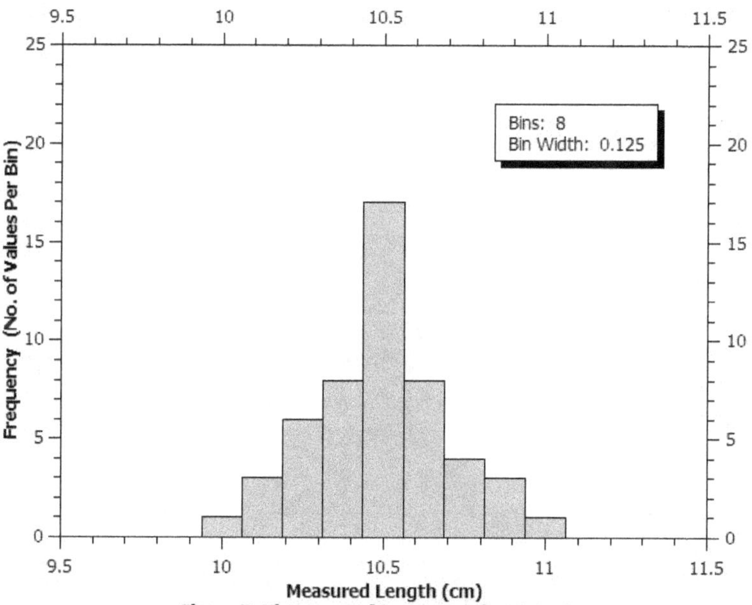

Figure 5. Histogram of Demonstration Data Set

15

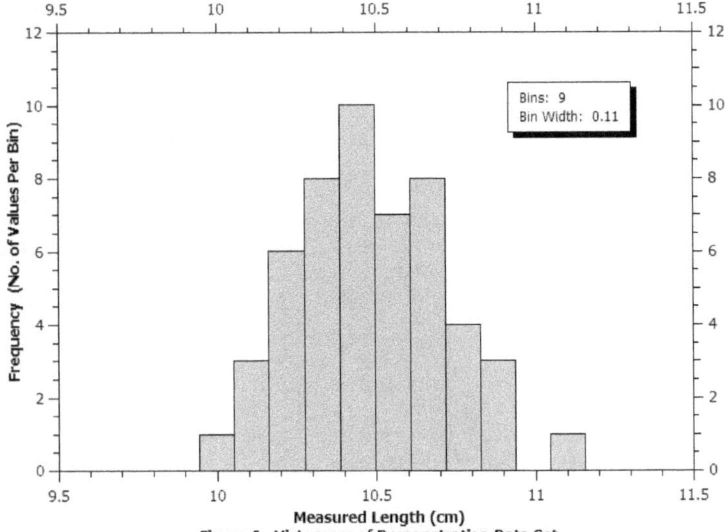

Figure 6. Histogram of Demonstration Data Set

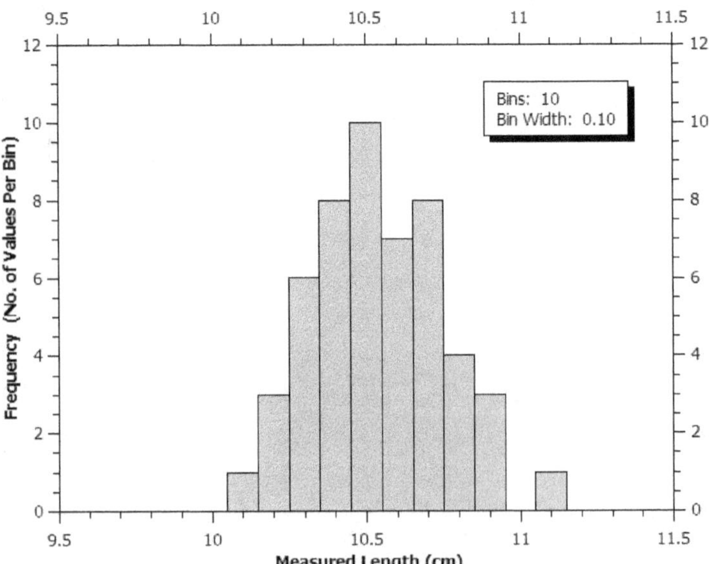

Figure 7. Histogram of Demonstration Data Set

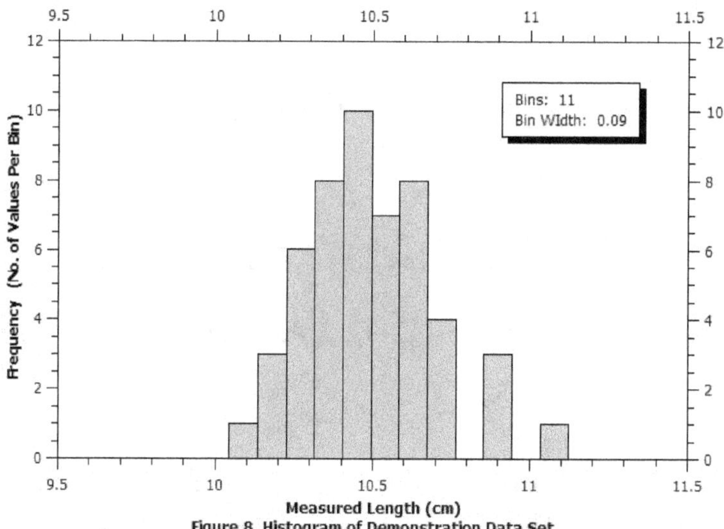

Figure 8. Histogram of Demonstration Data Set

Looking through the charts, the histogram with the numerically calculated optimal 7 bins did not show a good distribution of the data. The best distributions were obtained with 5, 9, and 10 bins. For the purpose of this discussion, the chart with 9 bins has been selected to represent the distribution of the data.

CHAPTER 6

The Mathematics Of the Normal Curve

The normal distribution, also known as the Gaussian distribution and the bell curve, is important because it describes many natural phenomena such as people's heights, blood pressure, IQ, etc.

The normal distribution is a Gaussian function given by the following equation

$$Y = \frac{1}{\sigma\sqrt{2\pi}} e^{\frac{-(x-\mu)^2}{2\sigma^2}} \qquad [4]$$

where

    Y = Value proportional to the probability of observing a given x-value

    σ = Standard deviation of the data population

    x = Data value

    μ = Mean of data population

To plot a probability density curve, the bin width must be taken into consideration. This is done by multiplying the Gaussian normal distribution function by the bin width, as follows

$$Y_P = Y * BW = \frac{1}{\sigma\sqrt{2\pi}} e^{\frac{-(x-\mu)^2}{2\sigma^2}} * BW \qquad [5]$$

where

Y_P = Probability of observing a given x-value

The probability density curve is a symmetrical, bell-shaped curve centered about the mean of the data population. The area under the curve drawn from -∞ to +∞ equals 1.0 and each Y_P-value gives the probability of observing a given x-value.

Figure 9 shows a normal probability density curve for the demonstration data set given in Table A1 using a bin width of 0.11 (9 bins).

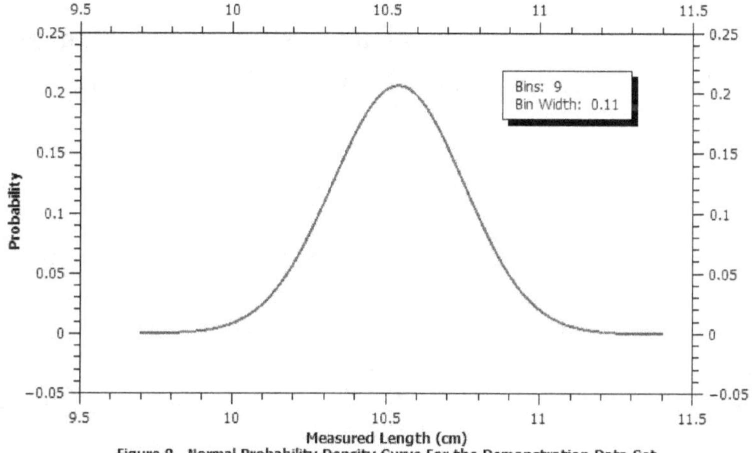

Figure 9. Normal Probability Density Curve For the Demonstration Data Set

What is needed to superimpose a normal plot over a histogram is a frequency distribution function curve where each y-value gives the projected number of values falling within each bin of the histogram. This curve (Y_f) is obtained by multiplying the probability density function (Y_P) by the total number of data points in the data set (N). Thus, the normal frequency distribution curve is given by

$$Y_f = Y_P * N = \frac{1}{\sigma\sqrt{2\pi}} e^{\frac{-(x-\mu)^2}{2\sigma^2}} * BW * N \qquad [6]$$

where

> Y_f = Frequency (i.e. the number of values falling within one bin centered on the given x-value)
> x = x-value at the center of a bin
> μ = Mean of data population
> σ = Standard deviation of the data population
> BW = Bin width
> N = Total number of data points in the data set

Figure 10 shows the frequency distribution function plot of the demonstration data set using a bin width of 0.11 (9 bins).

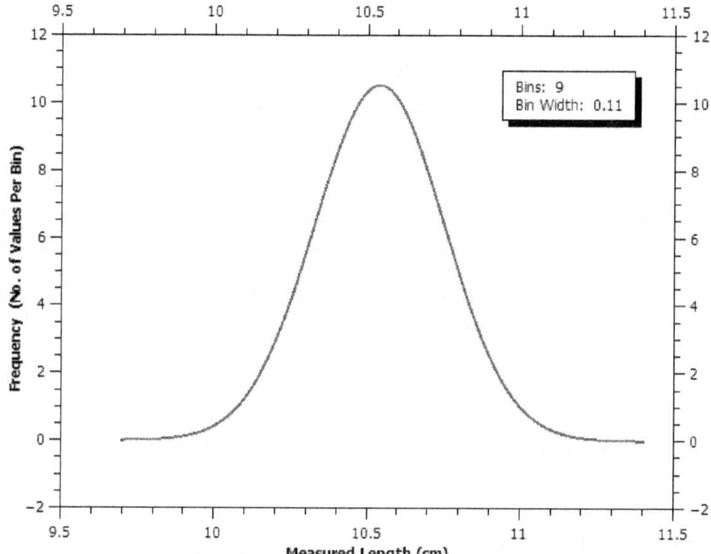

Figure 10. Normal Frequency Distribution Curve For the Demonstration Data Set

CHAPTER 7

Adding a Normal Curve To a Histogram

There are two ways of adding a normal frequency distribution curve to a histogram. One is to plot frequency values calculated from the data set being analyzed. The other is to plot a function curve.

Method 1- Plotting Calculated Frequency Values

Let's first look at how to plot a normal frequency distribution curve using calculated frequency values.

Table A2 gives the calculated frequency values used to plot the normal curve. The x-values used in the calculations were centered on the mean of the demonstration data set and covered the range of approximately +/-4 σ from the mean so that the entire normal curve would be displayed on the histogram. A bin width of 0.11 was used in the calculations, based on 9 bins over the range of the actual data (i.e. 10.1 - 11.1). Each x-value represents the center of a bin and is separated from the next x-value by one bin width.

Table A2: Calculated Probability and Frequency Values For the Demonstration Data Set Used To Plot the Normal Curve

n	x-Value at Center of Bin	z-Value at Center of Bin	Calculated Gaussian Function Values (Y)	Calculated Probability For Each Bin (Y*)	Calculated Frequency For Each Bin (Y₁)
1	9.66	-4.13	0.0003648	0.00004013	0.0020
2	9.77	-3.62	0.002708	0.0002978	0.0152
3	9.88	-3.10	0.01538	0.001692	0.0863
4	9.99	-2.58	0.06685	0.007353	0.3750
5	10.1	-2.07	0.2224	0.02446	1.2475
6	10.21	-1.55	0.5660	0.06227	3.1756
7	10.32	-1.03	1.1028	0.1213	6.1865
8	10.43	-0.51	1.6441	0.1805	9.2233
9	10.54	0.00	1.8758	0.2063	10.5232
10	10.65	0.52	1.6378	0.1802	9.1882
11	10.76	1.04	1.0944	0.1204	6.1395
12	10.87	1.56	0.5596	0.0616	3.1395
13	10.98	2.07	0.2190	0.0241	1.2286
14	11.09	2.59	0.0656	0.007214	0.3679
15	11.20	3.11	0.01503	0.001653	0.0843
16	11.31	3.62	0.002636	0.0002900	0.0148
17	11.42	4.14	0.0003538	0.00003892	0.001985
SUM:				1.00	51.0

The z-values shown in the table are given by

$$z = \frac{(x - \mu)}{\sigma} \tag{7}$$

and give the number of standard deviations each data point (x-value) is away from the mean. For now, the z-values are just used to show that our calculations cover the range of approximately +/-4σ but this parameter will be covered more later on in the discussion about the standard normal curve.

At the bottom of the table are summations of the calculated probabilities and frequencies for all of the bins over the range of approximately +/-4σ. These summations effectively represent the area under the probability density and frequency distribution curves, respectively. As expected, the probabilities add up to 1.0 while the frequencies add up to 51, the total number of data points in the data set.

To add this curve to the histogram in QtiPlot, proceed as follows:

Create a new chart table using the menu selection: "File \ New \ Table." This will open Chart Table 2.

In Column 1(X) of the new table, add the x-values used in the calculations (i.e. the values in the second column in Table A2 above). In Column 2(Y), add the calculated frequency values (i.e. the values in the last column of Table A2 above).

Double click on the small box containing the number (1) in the upper left hand corner of the histogram chart. This will open the "Add/Remove Curve" dialog box.

Using the "New Curves Style" drop-down box, select the desired style for the normal curve. Typically this will be either line, scatter, or line + symbol. For this example, we will choose Line + Symbol but note that this value can be easily changed later, if desired.

Next, click on the triangle next to "Table 2" in the "Available Data" section to expand it. Click on "Table 2_2," which represents the 2(Y) column of data in Chart Table 2, to select it and then click on the right arrow in the center of the dialog box to move it to the "Graph Contents" section. This adds the curve to the chart.

You may now need to rescale the x-axis of the chart in the same manner as described previously. Again, a good range for this particular chart is 9.5 to 11.5.

When done, click "OK" at the bottom of the dialog box to save your changes and close the dialog box.

If you want to change the color or style of the normal curve, double click on the top of the curve to open the "Plot Details" dialog box. Use the "Line" tab to change the properties of the line. Use the "Symbol" tab to add or remove the symbol, change its shape or change its color.

Click on "Apply" at the bottom of the dialog box to see your changes. When done, close the dialog box by clicking on "OK" at the bottom of the dialog box.

Click on the "Graph Title," "X Axis Title," or "Y Axis Title" labels on the chart to change them, as desired.

The finished chart is shown in Figure 11.

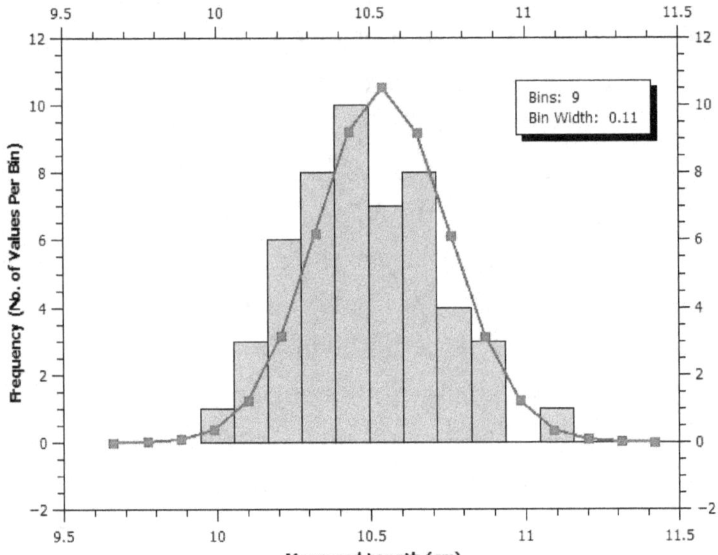

Figure 11. Histogram of Demonstration Data Set With Overlaid Calculated Normal Frequency Distribution Curve

Method 2 - Plotting a Function

The second method of adding a normal curve to a histogram is to plot the normal frequency distribution function on the graph. This is done as follows:

Click anywhere on the top part of the histogram chart to select it and then select "Graph \ Add Function..." from the top menu. This opens the "Add Function Curve" dialog box.

Type in the normal frequency distribution function equation (Equation 6) in the following format using numeric values for (N), (BW), (μ) and (σ):

$$(N*BW)*(1/(\sigma*sqrt(2*PI)))*exp(-(x-\mu\string^2)/(2*\sigma\string^2))$$

Here is how the equation would look for the demonstration data set.

26

$$51*0.11*(1/(0.2127*sqrt(2*PI)))*exp(-(x-10.539)^2/(2*0.2127^2))$$

Set the "From x " and "To x" parameters to define the range over which the curve will be plotted. In our case, the range would be 9.7 to 11.4 to cover +/- 4σ. Click on "Apply" to plot the curve and then "OK" to close the dialog box.

Here is the finished chart.

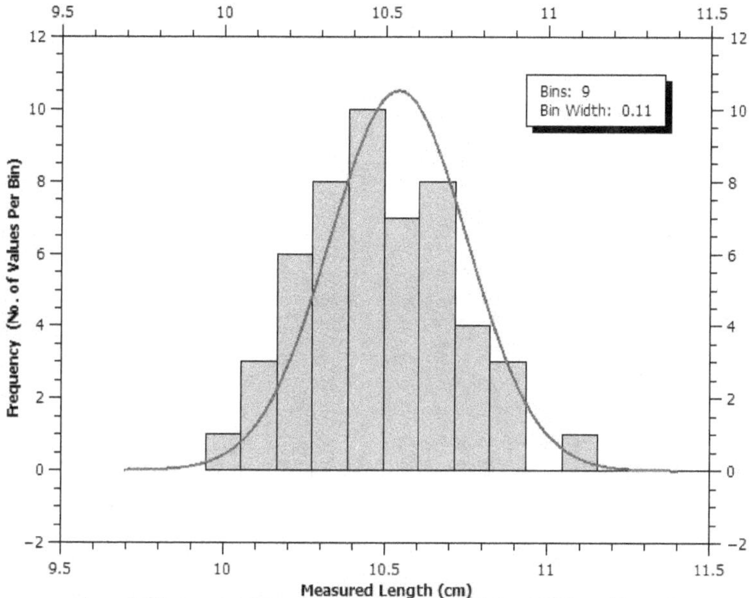

Figure 12. Histogram of Demonstration Data Set With Overlaid Normal Frequency Distribution Function Curve

Figure 13 shows the histogram with both the calculation-based normal curve and the function plot. As can be seen, the two normal curves are nearly identical except that the function plot is smoother because it uses a lot more data points.

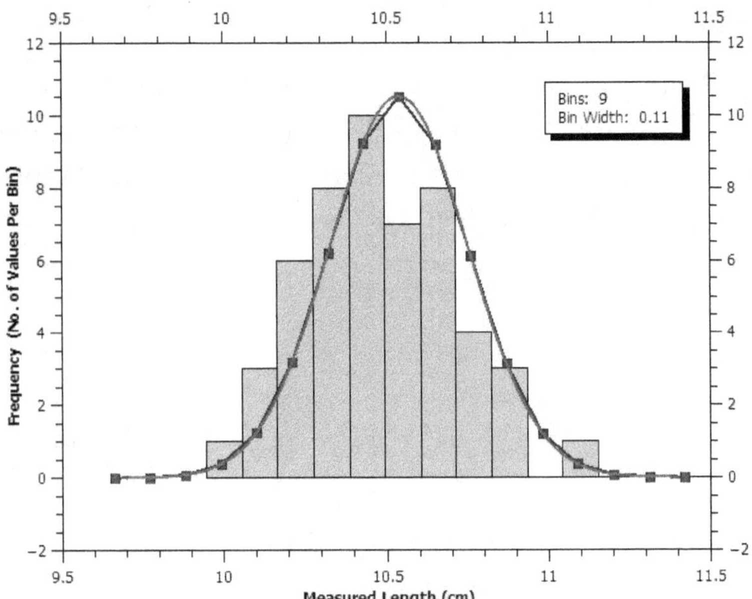

Figure 13. Histogram of Demonstration Data Set With Overlaid Calculated Normal
Frequency Distribution Curve and Normal Frequency Distribution Function Plot

CHAPTER 8

Adding a Standard Normal Curve To a Histogram

Sometimes it is desirable to plot the normal curve as a function of the standard deviation of the values rather than of the values themselves. This is done by standardizing the data with respect to the standard deviation.

By standardizing the data, all data sets can be presented in the same manner with a mean of zero and a standard deviation of one. This makes analysis of the date much easier since a single table of cumulative distribution values is sufficient to analyze any and all data sets.

Standardization is accomplished using the parameter (z), sometimes called the z-score or the Standard Score. This parameter was defined earlier (Equation 7) but is repeated here for convenience.

$$z = \frac{(x - \mu)}{\sigma} \qquad [7]$$

The standard normal distribution is obtained by substituting (z) into Equation 4, yielding:

$$Y_S = \frac{1}{\sqrt{2\pi}} e^{\frac{-z^2}{2}} \qquad\qquad [8]$$

The standard probability density function equation now becomes

$$Y_{PS} = Y_S * \frac{BW}{\sigma} = \frac{1}{\sqrt{2\pi}} e^{\frac{-z^2}{2}} * \frac{BW}{\sigma} \qquad\qquad [9]$$

and the standard frequency distribution function equation becomes

$$Y_{fS} = Y_S * \frac{BW}{\sigma} * N = Y_{PS} * N = \frac{1}{\sqrt{2\pi}} e^{\frac{-z^2}{2}} * \frac{BW}{\sigma} * N \qquad [10]$$

In the above three equations, the subscript (S) designates that the equations are standardized.

Also, in Equations 9 and 10, the bin width must be divided by the standard deviation to convert it to units of standard deviation (i.e. to standardize it). Thus the reason for the term (σ) in the denominator.

Finally, it should be noted that dividing (Y_S) by the standard deviation (σ) would yield Gaussian function values identical to those obtained with the non-standardized function (Y). It is not clear why this is not done but this is how the equation is presented in text books so we kept that notation here.

Table A3 gives the calculated probability and frequency values used to plot the standard normal curve. The x-values were the same as those used in the plotting of the non-standardized normal curve. Note that the calculated probabilities and frequencies are identical to those in Table A2 calculated using the non-standardized functions. This is as expected.

Table A3: Calculated Probability and Frequency Values For the Demonstration Data Set Used To Plot the Standard Normal Curve

n	x-Value at Center of Bin	z-Value at Center of Bin	Calculated Standard Gaussian Function Values (Y_s)	Calculated Probability For Each Bin (Y_{Ps})	Calculated Frequency For Each Bin (Y_{fs})
1	9.66	-4.13	0.00007759	0.00004013	0.00205
2	9.77	-3.62	0.0005758	0.0002978	0.0152
3	9.88	-3.10	0.003271	0.001692	0.0863
4	9.99	-2.58	0.01422	0.007353	0.3750
5	10.1	-2.07	0.04729	0.02446	1.2475
6	10.21	-1.55	0.1204	0.06227	3.1756
7	10.32	-1.03	0.2345	0.1213	6.1865
8	10.43	-0.51	0.3497	0.1805	9.2233
9	10.54	0.00	0.3989	0.2063	10.5232
10	10.65	0.52	0.3483	0.1802	9.1882
11	10.76	1.04	0.2328	0.1204	6.1395
12	10.87	1.56	0.1190	0.0616	3.1395
13	10.98	2.07	0.0466	0.0241	1.2286
14	11.09	2.59	0.0139	0.007214	0.3679
15	11.20	3.11	0.003197	0.001653	0.0843
16	11.31	3.62	0.0005607	0.0002900	0.0148
17	11.42	4.14	0.00007525	0.00003892	0.00198
SUM:				1.00	51.00

The Standard Normal Curve is now added to the histogram as follows:

Method 1- Plotting Calculated Frequency Values

To plot the standard normal frequency distribution curve on a histogram using calculated frequency values, create a new chart table in QtiPlot. Calculate the z-value for each x-value and paste the results into the 1(X) column of the new chart table. These values are given in Column 3 of Table A3 above for the demonstration data set. Next paste the calculated frequency values for each z-value into the 2(Y) column of the new chart table. These values are given in Column 6 of Table A3 above.

Double click on the small square with the number (1) in it at the upper left of the histogram chart to open the "Add/Remove Curves" dialog box. Select the style from the "New Curves Style" drop-down box, click on Table 2_2 representing column 2(Y) of the new chart table, and then click on the green right arrow in the center of the dialog box to move the date into the "Graph Contents" section of the dialog box. This adds the curve to the histogram.

Click "OK" to close the Add/Remove Curves" dialog box.

If needed, adjust the sale of the bottom x-axis by double clicking on one of the numeric labels on the x-axis to open the "General Plot Options" dialog box and entering in the desired "From" and "To" values in the "Scale" tab for the "Bottom" axis. In our charts, these values would be 9.5 and 11.5, respectively. Click "OK" to close the dialog box when finished.

Double click on the top of the standard normal frequency distribution curve just added to open the "Plot Details" dialog box. Click on the "Axes" tab then on the x-Axis drop down box. Select "Top" to specify that the standard normal frequency distribution curve will be plotted using the top axis scale. Clock "OK" to close the dialog box.

Double click on one of the numeric labels on the top axis to open the "General Plot Options" dialog box. Click on the "Scale" tab and then on "Top" to indicate that the changes will be made to the top axis.

Enter in the "From" and "To" values for the top x-axis. These values must be based on the scale range used for the bottom x-axis. In our example, the bottom axis goes from 9.5 to 11.5. Since the top axis is based on z-values, we must calculate the z-values for 9.5 and 11.5 and use those values for the "To" and "From" settings. The z-value for 9.5 is -4.88 and 4.52 for 11.5. Thus, the "From" value will be -4.88 and the "To" value will be 4.52. Once the values are entered, click "Apply" to make sure everything looks OK.

Make sure that the bottom axis did not change its scale. Sometimes, for some unknown reason, QtiPlot will adjust both the top and bottom axes to the same range when new scaling is applied. If the bottom axis scaling did change, select "Bottom" on the left side of the dialog and enter in the "From" and "To" values for the bottom x-axis (9.5 and 11.5 in our example). Once both axes are scaled properly, click "OK" to close the dialog box.

The finished graph for the demonstration data set is shown in Figure 14.

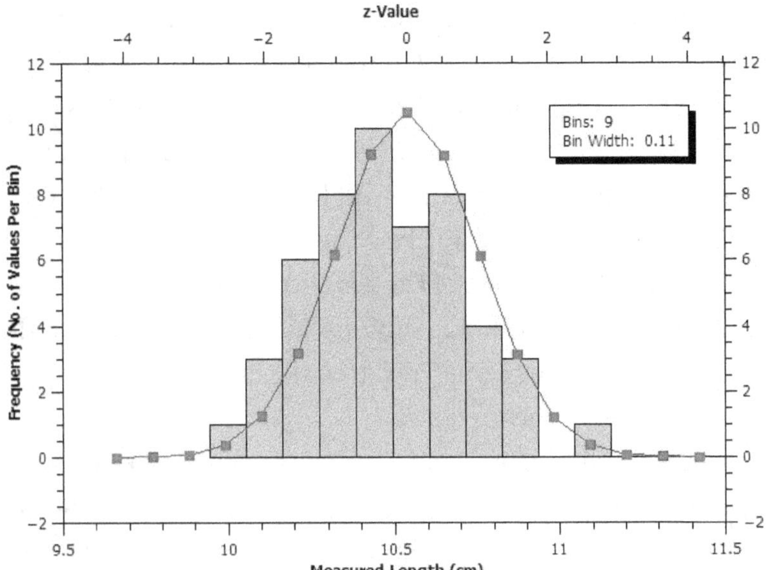

Figure 14. Histogram of Demonstration Data Set With Overlaid Calculated Standard Normal Frequency Distribution Curve

Method 2 - Plotting a Function

To plot the standard normal frequency distribution function on the chart, click on the top of the histogram chart to select it and then select "Graph / Add Function" from the top menu. Type in the standard normal frequency distribution function equation (Equation 10) in the following format using numeric values for (N), (BW) and (σ):

$$(N*BW/\sigma)*(1/(sqrt(2*PI)))*exp(-x^2/2)$$

Note that (x) is substituted for (z) in the formula because (x) is the variable used in the calculations by QtiPlot.

For our example, this equation becomes.

$$(51*0.11/0.2127)*(1/(sqrt(2*PI)))*exp(-x^2/2)$$

Enter the "From x" and "To x" values to define the range over which the curve will be plotted. In our case, the range would be -4.0 to 4.0 to cover +/- 4σ. Click on "Apply" to plot the function and then "OK" to close the dialog box. In many cases, depending on the range of the data set being evaluated, the x-axis will rescale so that both the histogram and the function plot will appear on the chart.

Double click on the top of the Standard Normal Distribution Function Curve to open the "Plot Details" dialog box, click on the "Axis" tab and from the drop-down box for the x-axis, select "Top" to designate the top axis scale for the curve.

Click "Apply" and then "OK" to close the dialog box.

Next, double click on a numeric label on the top axis to open the "General Plot Options" dialog box. Click on the "Scale" tab, select "Top" from the left side of the dialog box and enter in the "From" and "To" values. These should be the z-values for the range of the bottom x-axis. In our example, the bottom x-axis range is from 9.5 to 11.5 and the corresponding z-values values for the top axis are -4.88 and 4.52, respectively. Click "Apply" to apply the new scaling.

Finally, check the x-axis scale. If it has changed, reset it to the correct range. Once both axes are scaled properly, click "OK" to close the dialog box.

The finished chart for our example is shown in Figure 15.

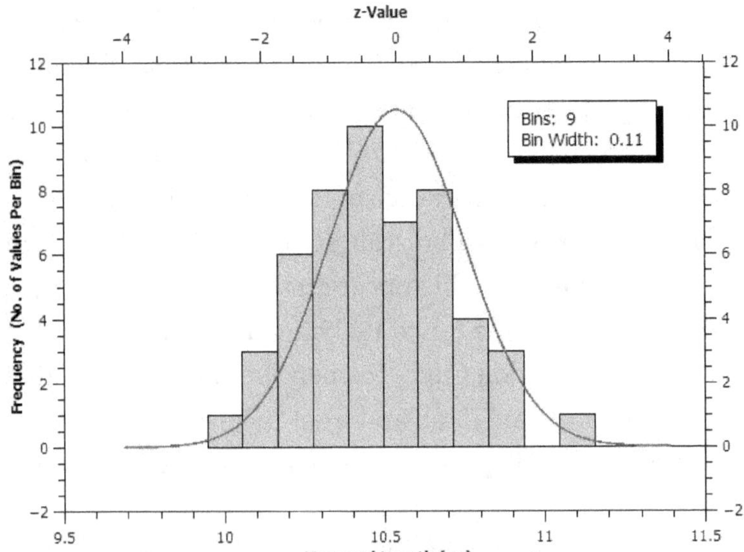

Figure 15. Histogram of Demonstration Data Set With Overlaid Standard Normal
Frequency Distribution Function Curve

CHAPTER 9

Summing Up

Using the techniques given in this discussion along with the free charting software, QtiPlot, you can now create professional quality histograms with overlaid normal curves.

No longer are you at the mercy of the limitations of Excel or statistical programs or forced to settle for ugly looking charts. You can now make the charts look exactly how you want them to look and use them with pride in your reports and publications.

QtiPlot is also suitable for creating a wide range of other types of scientific charts. If you are unable to get access to Origin, I highly recommend QtiPlot for all of your scientific charting needs, especially when you need great looking charts. Like I said earlier, it is a little clunky, but it will serve you well.

ABOUT THE AUTHOR

Walter Ebner is a retired scientist who has spent his entire career in the battery industry, much of it dedicated to conducting research on lithium and lithium-ion battery technologies. He has co-authored 23 professional papers and has over 10 patents.

Over the years, Walter has accumulated a lot of knowledge and developed a lot of tools to assist in his research that he would now like to pass on to others.

This is the first of many books that Walter plans to write. Hopefully, you've found it useful.